slow Cooker

slow Cooker

Amazing meals with minimum effort

Linda Doeser

p

This is a Parragon Publishing Book
This edition published in 2006

Parragon Publishing
Queen Street House
4 Queen Street
Bath
BA1 1HE, UK

ISBN: 1-40545-119-X

Printed in China

Author: Linda Doeser
Editor: Fiona Biggs
Designed by Fiona Roberts
Photography: Karen Thomas
Home Economist: Valerie Berry

Notes for the Reader

This book uses both imperial and US cup measurements. All spoon measurements are level; teaspoons are assumed to be 5 ml and tablespoons are assumed to be 15 ml. Unless otherwise stated, milk is assumed to be full fat, individual vegetables such as potatoes are medium, and pepper is freshly ground black pepper. Recipes using raw or very lightly cooked eggs should be avoided by infants, the elderly, pregnant women, convalescents and anyone suffering from an illness. Pregnant and breastfeeding women are advised to avoid eating peanuts and peanut products. The times given are an approximate guide only. Preparation times differ according to the techniques used by different people and the cooking times may also vary from those given. Optional ingredients, variations, or serving suggestions have not been included in the calculations.

Contents

INTRODUCTION

Slow cooking is not a new concept. There are hundreds of traditional slow-cooked dishes from all around the world, ranging from Tuscan stufato to Boston baked beans.

All kinds of containers have been contrived for just this purpose over the centuries, from the Maori hangi, an earth pit used to cook fabulous feasts, to the hay box, beloved of a generation of boy scouts. The electric slow cooker first appeared in the United States and Europe some thirty years ago and was intended to make this delicious method of cooking easier, more convenient, and less expensive.

The designers of today's new generation of slow cookers have developed and improved the original idea with the needs and demands of a twenty-first-century lifestyle in mind. There are so many conflicting calls on our time that preparing homecooked meals has become increasingly difficult. It's not even always possible to know what time you and the rest of the family are going to get home. The slow cooker provides a healthier and more economical solution than ready-cooked meals or home deliveries, combined with all the flavor of freshly cooked food. Of course, you do have to spend a little time in the kitchen preparing ingredients, but once everything is in the pot, you can safely leave it to cook while you get on with the rest of your life. Because the slow cooker cooks at a low temperature for a long time, you don't have to worry about pans boiling dry and food being spoiled if you're slightly delayed.

The slow cooker is also invaluable when you are entertaining. You can arrange your preparation time more conveniently so that, for example, you can concentrate on decorating an elaborate dessert while the main course is quietly simmering to perfection. It is also useful at that tricky moment when your guests arrive and you want to chat, as you don't have to worry about what is happening in the kitchen. For more informal gatherings, the slow cooker is ideal for preparing hot snacks and great for rounding off an evening at the movies or theater with a late night supper.

Although it's wonderful to come home on a cold winter's evening to a welcoming pot of goulash or curry, the slow cooker is just as useful in the summer when the last thing you want to do is slave over a hot stove but the family has grown bored with endless plates of salad. In fact, in some ways, it's even more useful in the summer as it gives out very little heat while it's cooking so the kitchen remains cool and pleasant.

What's cooking?

Almost all kinds of foods can be cooked in a slow cooker. Hearty casseroles, stews, and soups remain the most popular choices, but you can also prepare appetizers, desserts, delicate items like fish, snacks, side dishes, small cuts of meat, and even hot punch or a wine cup for a party.

Slow cooking is the ideal way to prepare less expensive, less tender cuts of meat, such as braising steak and chicken thighs, as these benefit from prolonged cooking.

However, not every dish takes a whole day to cook. Some can be timed perfectly to be ready for lunch when you return from a morning's shopping or to provide an after-game snack on a Saturday afternoon.

The slow cooker is not just for meat-eaters. Vegetarian main courses and vegetable accompaniments can also be cooked this way. However, root vegetables in particular take a surprisingly long time—often longer than meat. It is the ideal method for cooking legumes as you need have no worries about a pan boiling over or boiling dry.

In fact, there is very little that can't be cooked in a slow cooker. Pasta is a notable exception as it needs to be boiled quite vigorously rather than gently simmered. This doesn't really present a problem as it cooks so rapidly in a conventional pan. However, if you do want to add pasta to a dish in the slow cooker, boil it first until it is nearly tender, then add it to the cooker for the last 20–30 minutes of the cooking time. Rice is somewhat similar. Again, as it cooks quite quickly, it makes an easy accompaniment. For dishes where rice is an integral part, such as paella or jambalaya, it's best to add cooked rather than raw rice for the last 30 minutes of cooking time.

Ingredients with a delicate texture cannot withstand prolonged cooking. Fish and shellfish, for example, will fall apart, so they are best added shortly before the end of cooking. Fish, raw and live shellfish take 30–60 minutes in a slow cooker, while cooked shrimp take 15–30 minutes.

In both cases, they should be cooked on the high setting. It's best to add mushrooms toward the end of the cooking time.

Types of cooker

A cooker with a 4-quart working capacity is ideal for most families. An oval cooker offers more flexibility than a round one as it can more easily accommodate small roasts, such as lamb shanks, or a whole fish.

Modern slow cookers usually have a removable ceramic cooking pot but in older models the cooking container was often fixed inside the outer casing, making them more awkward to wash as the base unit must never be immersed in water. The lids on modern models and some older ones are usually made of heatproof glass. This allows you to monitor progress without uncovering the food, which would lower the temperature.

The base unit is made of metal and may be encased in a heatproof material. Two or more feet ensure stability. The handles are also usually made from a cool-touch material.

The controls on modern cookers are usually in the form of a dial and may include several settings—typically, high, low, and auto, and some also include medium. There will also be an off position. There may be a light to indicate when the cooker is switched on. However, not all older cookers have an off position and must be switched off at the mains socket. They do have a high and low setting. It is essential to read the manufacturer's instructions carefully before using the cooker for the first time. These will explain the settings and safety features, as well as describing the methods for cleaning and general care of the cooker.

Using the slow cooker

Place the cooker on a level counter, making sure that the cord does not overhang the edge. Check that the control switch is in the off position before you plug the cooker into the mains socket.

If your cooker has a removable cooking pot, lift it out of the base unit when placing the ingredients in it to avoid spills and splashes which can damage the base unit. For the same reason, you should not fill the cooking pot more than about two-thirds full. When you're ready to use the cooker put the cooking pot back into position, fit the lid, and switch on. Do not switch the base unit on without the cooking pot in position. Never put food or liquid directly into the base unit.

Modern slow cookers work by building up the heat and then maintaining an even temperature. Some older cookers must be preheated (see the manufacturer's instructions). As the food cooks, liquid evaporates and condenses on the lid, forming a seal. You should not lift the lid off the cooker for at least the first half of the cooking time. Very often, it will not be necessary to raise the lid until you're ready to serve. Food cooked in a slow cooker rarely needs stirring.

When the cooker is on the low setting it is safe to leave it unattended. The high setting cooks about twice as fast as the low one and manufacturers recommend that you keep an eye on the food while it is cooking. If you want to cook on high and need to go out or you're cooking overnight, it is best to use the auto setting, if your slow cooker has one, because the cooker starts cooking on high and then switches to low.

When the food is cooked, switch the dial to the off position and unplug the cooker. Handle the cooking pot with oven mitts as it will be very hot. Let the base unit and the cooking pot cool completely before you clean them. The pot and lid should be washed in warm soapy water, rinsed, and dried, or washed in the dishwasher if suitable. The base unit usually requires nothing more than wiping with a soft, dry cloth. Do not immerse the base unit in water.

Preparing food

In general, ingredients can be prepared for cooking in a slow cooker in very much the same way as they are for cooking in the oven or on the stove. However, there are a few guidelines which are worth following.

Trim any visible fat from meat. You can also skim off excess grease with a skimmer or spoon after cooking. Meat and poultry look more attractive and retain more flavor if they are seared first. Cook in a little oil over medium heat, stirring and turning occasionally, until browned on all sides. This also helps to reduce fat as you can pour it off from the pan or drain the meat with a slotted spoon.

Cut root vegetables into small pieces, precook them for 5 minutes in a little oil, and place them in the base of the cooker to make sure that they are immersed in liquid.

Most dried legumes need to be soaked before cooking and some must be boiled vigorously for 15 minutes to destroy naturally occurring toxins. These include aduki, black, borlotti, and red kidney beans and black-eyed peas. Bring them to a boil in a pan, boil rapidly for 15 minutes, then drain, and rinse before cooking in the slow cooker. Soybeans require pre-boiling for 1 hour because they contain a substance that prevents the body from absorbing protein.

As there is less evaporation in the slow cooker than with conventional cooking, less liquid is required. However, some liquid is essential. To reach the optimum temperature as quickly as possible—essential for food safety—bring the liquid to a boil before adding it to the cooker. If the sauce is too thin, stir a little cornstarch (1–2 tablespoons) to a paste with some water, then stir it into the cooker. Turn the control switch to high and cook for 15 minutes more.

Dairy products are best added about 30 minutes before serving to avoid curdling.

Hints and tips

◎ Position the cooker well out of the reach of children and make sure that the electric cable does not hang down from the counter.

◎ Don't lift the lid and poke the food with a spoon during cooking as this will cause a rapid drop in temperature.

◎ The cooking times given in the recipes are guidelines but many factors can affect them. Older legumes, for example, take longer to cook than more recently harvested ones.

◎ Hot steam will rise out of the cooker when you remove the lid so don't peer into it, and risk scalding your face.

◎ Use oven mitts when you lift out the cooking pot at the end of cooking and place a mat underneath the pot.

◎ Check that food is cooked through. This is especially important with poultry for health reasons. Pierce the thickest part—if the juices run clear, it is cooked through.

◎ Don't put the pot down on a hot stove, and when you've finished don't put the lid in cold water.

◎ Don't use the slow cooker if any of it is damaged, including the cable and plug. A chip in the cooking pot makes a great breeding site for bacteria.

◎ Don't leave leftovers in the cooking pot. Reheat them in the oven or on the stove, not in the slow cooker.

◎ Don't use the slow cooker for thawing frozen food as this can be a health hazard.

◎ Make sure the cooking pot is dry before re-using it.

◎ Only fill the cooking pot about two-thirds full to allow room for expansion during cooking.

◎ If food has stuck to the cooking pot, fill it with warm soapy water and let soak. Don't use scouring pads or abrasives to clean the pot as these will scratch it and food will stick to the scratches next time you use it.

CHAPTER 1: SIMPLE APPETIZERS AND SNACKS

GREEK BEAN & VEGETABLE SOUP

A great first course, this colorful country soup also makes a delicious light lunch served with poppy seed bread.

 Serves 4–6

 Preparation time: 15 minutes, plus overnight soaking

 Cooking time: 12 hours

Ingredients

2¾ cups dried navy beans, soaked in cold water overnight

2 onions, finely chopped

2 garlic cloves, finely chopped

2 potatoes, chopped

2 carrots, chopped

2 tomatoes, peeled and chopped

2 celery stalks, chopped

4 tbsp extra virgin olive oil

1 bay leaf

salt and pepper

To garnish

12 black olives

2 tbsp chopped fresh chives

1 Drain the beans and rinse well under cold running water. Place them in the slow cooker and add the onions, garlic, potatoes, carrots, tomatoes, celery, olive oil, and bay leaf.

2 Pour in 8¾ cups boiling water, making sure that all the ingredients are fully submerged. Cover and cook on low for 12 hours until the beans are tender.

3 Remove and discard the bay leaf. Season the soup to taste with salt and pepper and stir in the olives and chives. Ladle into warm soup bowls and serve.

Cook's tip
Navy beans do not need to be vigorously boiled for 15 minutes at the beginning of cooking.

Variation
For a more substantial soup, add a meaty cured ham bone with the other ingredients in step 1. Before serving, remove the bone, cut off the meat, and return it to the soup.

CHICKEN & LEEK SOUP

This is a two-for-the-price-of-one dish as you can serve the broth
as a first course and serve the chicken for the main course.

 Serves 6–8

Preparation time: 15 minutes, plus 7 hours' soaking

Cooking time: 7½ hours

Ingredients

12 prunes, pitted, or 12 no-soak prunes

4 chicken portions

4 cups sliced leeks

6¼ cups hot chicken or beef stock

1 bouquet garni

salt and pepper

1 If using ordinary prunes, place them in a bowl and add cold water to cover. Let soak while
the soup is cooking.

2 Place the chicken portions and leeks in the slow cooker. Pour in the stock and add the bouquet garni.
Cover and cook on low for 7 hours.

3 If you are going to serve the chicken with the soup, remove it from the cooker with a slotted spoon and
cut the meat off the bones. Cut it into bite-size pieces and return it to the cooker. Otherwise, leave the
chicken portions in the slow cooker.

4 Drain the prunes, if necessary. Add the prunes to the soup and season to taste with salt and pepper.
Re-cover and cook on high for 30 minutes.

5 Remove and discard the bouquet garni. Either ladle the soup, including the cut-up chicken, into warm
bowls or remove the chicken portions and keep warm for the main course, then ladle the broth into warm
bowls. Serve immediately.

Cook's tip
*Home-made stock is always best, but you can use good-
quality bouillon cubes or bouillon powder. Be careful when
seasoning the soup as bouillon cubes may be extra salty.*

Variation
*For a variation of this recipe you can replace half the
chicken with 1 lb 4 oz stewing beef in a single piece. Tie
it with string to keep it in shape. Cut it into pieces with the
chicken and return to the soup.*

TEX-MEX BEAN DIP

Not only is this spicy warm dip a tasty appetizer, but it is also an ideal party snack. Serve it with a selection of dippers if you like.

Serves 4

Preparation time: 15 minutes, plus 5 minutes' pre-cooking

Cooking time: 2 hours

Ingredients

2 tbsp corn oil

1 onion, finely chopped

2 garlic cloves, finely chopped

2–3 fresh green chilies, seeded
  and finely chopped

14 oz canned refried beans
  or red kidney beans

2 tbsp chili sauce or taco sauce

6 tbsp hot vegetable stock

1 cup grated Cheddar cheese, grated

salt and pepper

1 fresh red chili, seeded and
  shredded, to garnish

tortilla chips, to serve

1 Heat the oil in a large, heavy skillet. Add the onion, garlic, and chilies and cook, stirring occasionally, over low heat for 5 minutes until the onion is soft and translucent. Transfer the mixture to the slow cooker.

2 Add the refried beans to the slow cooker. If using red kidney beans, drain well and rinse under cold running water. Reserve 2 tablespoons of the beans and mash the remainder coarsely with a potato masher. Add all the beans to the slow cooker.

3 Add the sauce, hot stock, and grated cheese, season with salt and pepper, and stir well. Cover and cook on low for 2 hours.

4 Transfer the dip to a serving bowl, garnish with shredded red chili, and serve warm with tortilla chips on the side.

Cook's tip
*Chilies vary considerably in their degree of hotness.
As a general rule, small pointed chilies tend to be
hotter than larger blunt ones, but even pods from
the same plant can vary.*

Louisiana Zucchini

An attractive vegetarian appetizer, this lightly spiced dish can also be served as an accompaniment to chicken or simply broiled fish.

Serves 6

Preparation time: 15 minutes

Cooking time: 2 ½ hours

Ingredients

2 lb 4 oz zucchini, thickly sliced

1 onion, finely chopped

2 garlic cloves, finely chopped

2 red bell peppers, seeded and chopped

5 tbsp hot vegetable stock

4 tomatoes, peeled and chopped

2 tbsp butter, diced

salt and cayenne pepper

3 tbsp chopped fresh parsley, to garnish

1 Place the zucchini, onion, garlic, and bell peppers in the slow cooker and season to taste with salt and cayenne pepper. Pour in the stock and mix well.

2 Sprinkle the chopped tomato on top and dot with the butter. Cover and cook on high for 2 ½ hours until tender. Garnish with the parsley and serve.

Cook's tip

To peel tomatoes, score a cross in the bottom end and place in a heatproof bowl. Pour in boiling water to cover and let stand for 30–60 seconds. Drain and refresh under cold water. The skins will then peel off easily.

Variation

Replace half the zucchini with patty pan squash and substitute a mixture of 4 tablespoons uncolored dry bread crumbs and 4 tablespoons grated Parmesan cheese for the tomatoes. Cover and cook on low for 6 hours.

SWEET-AND-SOUR CHICKEN WINGS

Messy but delicious, chicken wings are also good to serve as party nibbles—just increase the quantity.

 Serves 4–6

Preparation time: 10 minutes, plus 10 minutes for the sauce

Cooking time: 5 hours

Ingredients

1 lb 4 oz chicken wings, tips removed

2 celery stalks, chopped

3 cups hot chicken stock

2 tbsp cornstarch

3 tbsp white wine vinegar or rice vinegar

3 tbsp dark soy sauce

5 tbsp sweet chili sauce

1/4 cup soft brown sugar

14 oz canned pineapple
  chunks in juice, drained

7 oz canned sliced bamboo
  shoots, drained and rinsed

1/2 green bell pepper, seeded and thinly sliced

1/2 red bell pepper, seeded and thinly sliced

salt

1 Put the chicken wings and celery in the slow cooker and season with salt. Pour in the chicken stock, cover, and cook on low for 5 hours.

2 Drain the chicken wings, reserving 1 1/2 cups of the stock, and keep warm. Pour the reserved stock into a pan and stir in the cornstarch. Add the vinegar, soy sauce, and chili sauce. Place over a medium heat and stir in the sugar. Cook, stirring constantly, for 5 minutes, or until the sugar has dissolved completely and the sauce is thickened, smooth, and clear.

3 Lower the heat, stir in the pineapple, bamboo shoots, and bell peppers and simmer gently for 2–3 minutes. Stir in the chicken wings until they are thoroughly coated, then transfer to a serving platter.

Variation
You can add other flavorings to the sauce if you like, but make sure that they are all very thinly sliced so that they cook quickly. Try strips of carrot and fresh ginger root.

CHAPTER 2: EVERYDAY MEALS

TRADITIONAL POT ROAST

*There is something almost magical about coming home on a cold day
to a tender beef pot roast and all its accompanying vegetables.*

Serves 6

Preparation time: 20 minutes

Cooking time: 9–10 hours

Ingredients

1 onion, finely chopped

4 carrots, sliced

4 baby turnips sliced

4 celery stalks, sliced

2 potatoes, peeled and sliced

1 sweet potato, peeled and sliced

3–4 lb beef pot roast

1 bouquet garni

1 ¼ cups hot beef stock

salt and pepper

1 Place the onion, carrots, turnips, celery, potatoes, and sweet potato in the slow cooker and stir to
mix well.

2 Rub the beef all over with salt and pepper, then place on top of the bed of vegetables. Add the
bouquet garni and pour in the stock. Cover and cook on low for 9–10 hours, until the beef is cooked
to your liking.

3 Remove the beef, carve into slices, and arrange on serving plates. Spoon some of the vegetables
and cooking juices onto the plates and serve.

Cook's tip

*If you like thickened gravy, keep the meat and vegetables
warm, transfer the cooking juices to a small pan, and
place over low heat. Stir 1 tablespoon cornstarch with
2 tablespoons water to make a paste, stir into the cooking
juices, and bring to a boil, stirring constantly, until thick.*

Variation

*You can add or substitute all kinds of vegetables to this
traditional, but basic recipe. For example, you could
substitute 2 sliced leeks for the onion and rutabaga for the
turnips. You could also replace half the beef stock with
red wine, if you like.*

CHICKEN STEW

Nothing is nicer on a cold winter's evening than sitting down to this hearty, one-pot dish.

Serves 4

Preparation time: 20 minutes, plus 10 minutes' pre-cooking

Cooking time: 7 hours

Ingredients

3 tbsp corn oil

1 large onion, thinly sliced

1 green bell pepper, seeded and chopped

8 chicken pieces, such as thighs
  and drumsticks

14 oz canned chopped tomatoes, drained

pinch of cayenne pepper

1 tbsp Worcestershire sauce

1 1/4 cups hot chicken stock

1 tbsp cornstarch

generous 1 cup frozen corn, thawed

generous 3 cups frozen fava beans, thawed

salt

crusty bread, to serve

1 Heat the oil in a large, heavy skillet. Add the onion and bell pepper and cook over medium heat, stirring occasionally, for 5 minutes until the onion is softened. Using a slotted spoon, transfer the mixture to the slow cooker.

2 Add the chicken to the skillet and cook, turning occasionally, for 5 minutes until golden all over. Transfer to the slow cooker and add the tomatoes. Season with a pinch of cayenne pepper and salt. Stir the Worcestershire sauce into the hot stock and pour into the slow cooker. Cover and cook on low for 6 1/2 hours.

3 Mix the cornstarch to a paste with 2–3 tablespoons water and stir into the stew. Add the corn and beans, re-cover, and cook on high for 30–40 minutes until everything is cooked through and piping hot. Transfer to warm plates and serve with crusty bread.

Variation
If you like, you can use canned corn and fava beans. Drain well and rinse under cold water, then drain again.

NUTTY CHICKEN

*Chicken simmers to tender perfection in a rich sauce flavored
with walnuts, lemon, ginger, and, surprisingly, molasses.*

 Serves 4

Preparation time: 15 minutes, plus 10–15 minutes' pre-cooking

Cooking time: 6 hours

Ingredients

3 tbsp sunflower oil

4 skinless chicken portions

2 shallots, chopped

1 tsp ground ginger

1 tbsp all-purpose flour

scant 2 cups beef stock

½ cup walnut pieces

grated rind of 1 lemon

2 tbsp lemon juice

1 tbsp molasses

salt and pepper

fresh watercress or mizuna sprigs, to garnish

1 Heat the oil in a large, heavy skillet. Season the chicken portions with salt and pepper and add to the skillet. Cook over medium heat, turning occasionally, for 5–8 minutes, until lightly golden all over. Transfer to the slow cooker.

2 Add the shallots to the skillet and cook, stirring occasionally, for 3–4 minutes until softened. Sprinkle in the ginger and flour and cook, stirring constantly, for 1 minute. Gradually stir in the stock and bring to a boil, stirring constantly. Lower the heat and simmer for 1 minute, then stir in the nuts, lemon rind and juice, and molasses.

3 Pour the sauce over the chicken. Cover and cook on low for 6 hours until the chicken is cooked through and tender. Taste and adjust the seasoning if necessary. Transfer the chicken to warm plates, spoon some of the sauce over each portion, garnish with watercress sprigs, and serve immediately.

Variation
*If you prefer you can use pecans instead of
walnuts and lime instead of lemon.*

GOULASH

There are many versions of this traditional beef stew, which dates back to the ninth century. Finishing it with sour cream is, however, a modern addition.

Serves 4

Preparation time: 20 minutes, plus 25 minutes' pre-cooking

Cooking time: 9 hours

Ingredients

4 tbsp sunflower oil

1 lb 7 oz braising steak, cut
  into 1-inch cubes

2 tsp all-purpose flour

2 tsp paprika

1 1/2 cups beef stock

3 onions, chopped

4 carrots, diced

1 large potato or 2 medium potatoes, diced

1 bay leaf

1/2–1 tsp caraway seeds

14 oz canned chopped tomatoes

2 tbsp sour cream

salt and pepper

1 Heat half the oil in a heavy skillet. Add the beef and cook over medium heat, stirring frequently, until browned all over. Lower the heat and stir in the flour and paprika. Cook, stirring constantly, for 2 minutes. Gradually stir in the stock and bring to a boil, then transfer the mixture to the slow cooker.

2 Rinse out the skillet and heat the remaining oil in it. Add the onions and cook over low heat, stirring occasionally, for 5 minutes until softened. Stir in the carrots and potato and cook for a few minutes more. Add the bay leaf, caraway seeds, and tomatoes with their can juices. Season with salt and pepper.

3 Transfer the vegetable mixture to the slow cooker, stir well, then cover, and cook on low for 9 hours until the meat is tender.

4 Remove and discard the bay leaf. Stir in the sour cream and serve immediately.

Cook's tip
Use sweet Hungarian paprika for the best flavor. Caraway seeds have a highly distinctive taste a little like aniseed, so you may want to adjust the quantity or even omit them altogether.

MEXICAN PORK CHOPS

Pork is traditionally served with sharp-flavored fruit to counterbalance its richness.
This unusual and refreshing recipe uses pineapple to do this.

 Serves 4

Preparation time: 15 minutes, plus 10 minutes' pre-cooking

Cooking time: 6¼ hours

Ingredients

4 pork chops, trimmed of excess fat

2 tbsp corn oil

1 lb canned pineapple cubes in fruit juice

1 red bell pepper, seeded and finely chopped

2 fresh jalapeño chilies, seeded and
  finely chopped

1 onion, finely chopped

1 tbsp chopped fresh cilantro

½ cup hot chicken stock

salt and pepper

fresh cilantro sprigs, to garnish

1 Season the chops with salt and pepper. Heat the oil in a large, heavy skillet. Add the chops and cook over medium heat for 2–3 minutes each side until lightly browned. Transfer them to the slow cooker. Drain the pineapple, reserving the juice, and set aside.

2 Add the bell pepper, chilies, and onion to the skillet and cook, stirring occasionally, for 5 minutes until the onion is softened. Transfer the mixture to the slow cooker and add the cilantro and stock, together with ½ cup of the reserved pineapple juice. Cover and cook on low for 6 hours until the chops are tender.

3 Add the reserved pineapple to the slow cooker, re-cover, and cook on high for 15 minutes. Serve immediately, garnished with fresh cilantro sprigs.

Cook's tip
Jalapeño chilies are the best-known Mexican chilies and may be green or red. They are quite small, blunt, and fleshy, with a medium hot flavor.

Variation
You could substitute 1 lb 7 oz cubed boneless blade shoulder of pork for the chops and canned mandarin oranges for the pineapple.

CURED HAM COOKED IN CIDER

This is a great way to cook a family-size piece of cured ham as it prevents the meat from drying out and lets the delicious spicy flavors penetrate.

🍽 Serves 6

🥣 Preparation time: 10 minutes, plus 15 minutes' standing

🧤 Cooking time: 8 hours

Ingredients

2 lb 4 oz boneless cured ham in a single piece

1 onion, halved

4 cloves

6 black peppercorns

1 tsp juniper berries

1 celery stalk, chopped

1 carrot, sliced

3 cups hard cider

fresh vegetables, such as mashed
   potatoes and peas, to serve

1 Place a trivet or rack in the slow cooker, if you like, and stand the ham on it. Otherwise, just place the ham in the cooker. Stud each of the onion halves with 2 cloves and add to the cooker with the peppercorns, juniper berries, celery, and carrot.

2 Pour in the hard cider, cover, and cook on low for 8 hours until the meat is tender.

3 Remove the ham from the cooker and place on a board. Tent with foil and let stand for 10–15 minutes. Discard the cooking liquid and flavorings.

4 Cut off any rind and fat from the ham, then carve into slices, and serve with fresh vegetables.

Cook's tip
However large cuts of meat are cooked, including in the slow cooker, they benefit from being allowed to stand before carving. This evens up the texture of the meat so it is easier to carve into neat slices. Loosely covering the ham with foil keeps it hot.

SAUSAGE & BEAN STEW

This is an inexpensive and easy dish—plus it is very good on a cold evening.

Serves 4

Preparation time: 10 minutes, plus 10 minutes' pre-cooking

Cooking time: 6 hours

Ingredients

2 tbsp sunflower oil

2 onions, chopped

2 garlic cloves, finely
  chopped

2/3 cup chopped bacon

1 lb 2 oz pork sausage links

14 oz canned navy beans, red kidney beans, or
  black-eyed peas, drained and rinsed

2 tbsp chopped fresh parsley

2/3 cup hot beef stock

To serve

4 slices French bread

1/2 cup grated Swiss cheese

1 Heat the oil in a heavy skillet. Add the onions and cook over low heat, stirring occasionally, for 5 minutes until softened. Add the garlic, bacon, and sausage links, and cook, stirring and turning the sausages occasionally, for 5 minutes more.

2 Using a slotted spoon, transfer the mixture from the skillet to the slow cooker. Add the beans, parsley, and beef stock, then cover, and cook on low for 6 hours.

3 Just before serving, lightly toast the bread under a preheated broiler. Divide the grated cheese among the toast slices and place under the broiler until just melted.

4 Ladle the cassoulet onto warm plates, top each portion with the cheese-toast, and serve.

Cook's tip
For the best results, use top-quality sausages and for a special occasion, splash out on wild boar or venison sausages.

PORK WITH ALMONDS

*Olives, chilies, capers, and, of course, almonds provide a delicious
mix of flavors in this traditional Mexican stew.*

Serves 4

Preparation time: 25 minutes, plus 25 minutes' pre-cooking

Cooking time: 5 hours

Ingredients

2 tbsp corn or sunflower oil

2 onions, chopped

2 garlic cloves, finely chopped

2-inch cinnamon stick

3 cloves

1 cup ground almonds

1 lb 10 oz boneless pork,
   cut into 1-inch cubes

4 tomatoes, peeled and chopped

2 tbsp capers

1 cup green olives, pitted

3 pickled jalapeño chilies, drained,
   seeded, and cut into rings

1 ½ cups chicken stock

salt and pepper

fresh cilantro sprigs, to garnish (optional)

1 Heat half the oil in a large, heavy skillet. Add the onions and cook over low heat, stirring
occasionally, for 5 minutes until softened. Add the garlic, cinnamon, cloves, and almonds
and cook, stirring frequently, for 8–10 minutes. Be careful not to burn the almonds.

2 Remove and discard the spices and transfer the mixture to a food processor. Process to a smooth purée.

3 Rinse out the skillet and return to the heat. Heat the remaining oil, then add the pork, in batches if
necessary. Cook over medium heat, stirring frequently, for 5–10 minutes until browned all over. Return
all the pork to the skillet and add the almond purée, tomatoes, capers, olives, chilies, and chicken stock.
Bring to a boil, then transfer to the slow cooker.

4 Season with salt and pepper and mix well. Cover and cook on low for 5 hours. To serve, transfer to
warm plates and garnish with cilantro sprigs, if desired.

Cook's tip
*The small flower buds from the caper bush are sold
preserved in a mixture of salt and vinegar or in salt alone.
Pickled capers need to be rinsed, but those preserved in
salt alone can simply be brushed with your fingertips.*

TAGLIATELLE WITH SHRIMP

*This lovely summery dish is perfect for family suppers
and is special enough to serve to guests.*

Serves 4

Preparation time: 5 minutes

Cooking time: 7 1/4 hours

Ingredients

14 oz tomatoes, peeled
  and chopped

5 oz tomato paste

1 garlic clove, finely chopped

2 tbsp chopped fresh parsley

1 lb 2 oz cooked, peeled
  large shrimp

6 fresh basil leaves, torn

14 oz dried tagliatelle

salt and pepper

fresh basil leaves, to garnish

1 Put the tomatoes, tomato paste, garlic, and parsley in the slow cooker and season with salt and pepper.
Cover and cook on low for 7 hours.

2 Add the shrimp and basil. Re-cover and cook on high for 15 minutes.

3 Meanwhile, bring a large pan of lightly salted water to a boil. Add the pasta, bring back to a boil, and
cook for 10–12 minutes until tender but still firm to the bite.

4 Drain the pasta and tip it into a warm serving bowl. Add the shrimp sauce and toss lightly with 2 large
forks. Garnish with the basil leaves and serve immediately.

Cook's tip
*For the richest flavor, use sun-ripened tomatoes.
Those ripened under glass lack sweetness and tend
to be watery. If they're all that's available, you can
substitute canned chopped tomatoes instead.*

Variation
*Substitute 15 oz drained, canned clams
for the shrimp for tagliatelle alle vongole.*

VEGETABLE STEW WITH DUMPLINGS

This hearty, one-pot, vegetarian dish is simplicity itself, but if you're too tired to bother with the dumplings, just serve it with fresh crusty bread.

Serves 6

Preparation time: 20 minutes

Cooking time: 6½ hours

Ingredients

½ rutabaga, cut into chunks

2 onions, sliced

2 potatoes, cut into chunks

2 carrots, cut into chunks

2 celery stalks, sliced

2 zucchini, sliced

2 tbsp tomato paste

2½ cups hot vegetable stock

1 bay leaf

1 tsp ground coriander

½ tsp dried thyme

14 oz canned corn, drained

salt and pepper

For the parsley dumplings

1¾ cups self-rising flour

⅔ cup vegetable suet

2 tbsp chopped fresh parsley

½ cup milk

1 Put the rutabaga, onions, potatoes, carrots, celery, and zucchini into the slow cooker. Stir the tomato paste into the stock and pour it over the vegetables. Add the bay leaf, coriander, and thyme and season with salt and pepper. Cover and cook on low for 6 hours.

2 To make the dumplings, sift the flour with a pinch of salt into a bowl and stir in the suet and parsley. Add just enough milk to make a firm but light dough. Knead lightly and shape into 12 small balls.

3 Stir the corn into the vegetable casserole and place the dumplings on top. Cook on high for 30 minutes. Serve immediately.

Cook's tip
It can be quite tricky to cook vegetables well in a slow cooker and they can often take longer than you think. It's important, therefore, to cut them into even chunks of about the same size.

Variation
You can substitute or add whatever vegetables you like best. For example, swap leeks for the onions, a sweet potato for the ordinary potatoes, and fennel for the celery. If you like, substitute canned legumes, such as kidney beans or cannellini beans, for the corn.

BOSTON BAKED BEANS

This traditional New England dish can be served on its own with plenty of warm, fresh bread or as an accompaniment to roast pork.

Serves 4–6

Preparation time: 15 minutes, plus overnight soaking

Cooking time: 3 + 11 hours (14 hours in total)

Ingredients

2 ½ cups dried white haricot beans, soaked
   overnight in cold water and drained

4 oz salt pork, soaked in cold
   water for 3 hours and drained

1 onion, chopped

3 tbsp molasses

3 tbsp molasses sugar

2 tsp dry mustard

salt and pepper

1 Place the beans in the slow cooker and add about 6 ¼ cups boiling water so that they are covered. Cover and cook on high for 3 hours. Meanwhile, cut the salt pork into chunks.

2 Drain the beans, reserving 1 cup of the cooking liquid. Mix the reserved liquid with the molasses, sugar, mustard, and 1 teaspoon salt.

3 Return the beans to the slow cooker and add the salt pork, onion, and the molasses mixture. Stir, then cover, and cook on low for 11 hours.

4 Adjust the seasoning and serve immediately.

Cook's tip

Molasses is a by-product when sugar cane is refined. It is thick, dark, and very concentrated with a distinctively rich flavor. It is not so sweet as other syrups, and blackstrap molasses, in particular, has quite a bitter taste.

Variation

This was never intended as a vegetarian dish, but you could make a meatless version by omitting the salt pork and stirring in 1 cup grated Cheddar cheese at the end of cooking.

WARM GARBANZO BEAN SALAD

Garbanzos have a deliciously nutty flavour that works well with an herbed dressing.
They are notorious for taking ages to cook, so the slow cooker solves the problem.

Serves 6

Preparation time: 10 minutes

Cooking time: 12 hours

Ingredients

1 cup dried garbanzo beans, soaked overnight
   in cold water and drained

1 cup pitted black olives

4 scallions, finely chopped

fresh parsley sprigs, to garnish

crusty bread, to serve

For the dressing

2 tbsp red wine vinegar

2 tbsp mixed chopped fresh herbs, such
   as parsley, rosemary, and thyme

3 garlic cloves, very finely chopped

1/2 cup extra virgin olive oil

salt and pepper

1 Place the garbanzo beans in the slow cooker and add sufficient boiling water to cover. Cover and cook on low for 12 hours.

2 Drain well and transfer to a bowl. Stir in the olives and scallions.

3 To make the dressing, whisk together the vinegar, herbs, and garlic in a pitcher and season with salt and pepper to taste. Gradually whisk in the olive oil. Pour the dressing over the still-warm garbanzos and toss lightly to coat. Garnish with the parsley sprigs and serve warm with crusty bread.

Cook's tip
This also makes a tasty appetizer for 8–10 people. You
can make it in advance and serve cold, but not chilled.

CHAPTER 3: LOW FAT

VEGETABLE CURRY

*This is a wonderfully adaptable recipe that can be served
with other Indian dishes or simply with plain boiled rice.*

🍽 Serves 4–6

🥣 Preparation time: 15 minutes, plus 20 minutes' pre-cooking

🧤 Cooking time: 5 hours

Ingredients

2 tbsp vegetable oil

1 tsp cumin seeds

1 onion, sliced

2 curry leaves

1-inch piece fresh ginger root,
    finely chopped

2 fresh red chilies, seeded and chopped

2 tbsp curry paste

2 carrots, sliced

1 $\frac{1}{2}$ cups snow peas

1 cauliflower, cut into flowerets

3 tomatoes, peeled and chopped

$\frac{3}{4}$ cup frozen peas, thawed

$\frac{1}{2}$ tsp ground turmeric

$\frac{2}{3}$–1 cup hot vegetable
    or chicken stock

salt and pepper

1 Heat the oil in a large, heavy pan. Add the cumin seeds and cook, stirring constantly, for
1–2 minutes until they give off their aroma and begin to pop. Add the onion and curry leaves and
cook, stirring occasionally, for 5 minutes until the onion has softened. Add the ginger and chilies
and cook, stirring occasionally, for 1 minute.

2 Stir in the curry paste and cook, stirring, for 2 minutes, then add the carrots, snow peas, and cauliflower
flowerets. Cook for 5 minutes, then add the tomatoes, peas, and turmeric, and season with salt and
pepper. Cook for 3 minutes, then add $\frac{2}{3}$ cup of the stock, and bring to a boil.

3 Transfer the mixture to the slow cooker. If the vegetables are not covered, add more hot stock, then
cover, and cook on low for 5 hours until tender. Remove and discard the curry leaves before serving.

Cook's tip
*Curry leaves are used in Indian cooking in the same
way as bay leaves are used in Western dishes. They are
available from supermarkets and Indian stores, as too are
ready-made curry pastes. These pastes may be mild or hot.*

EASY CHINESE CHICKEN

This is simplicity itself, requiring very little preparation, yet it is packed with flavor and makes a great midweek supper.

Serves 4

Preparation time: 10 minutes, plus 5 minutes' pre-cooking

Cooking time: 4 hours

Ingredients

2 tsp grated fresh ginger root

4 garlic cloves, finely chopped

2 star anise

2/3 cup Chinese rice wine or
   medium dry sherry

2 tbsp dark soy sauce

1 tsp sesame oil

4 skinless chicken thighs or drumsticks

shredded scallions, to garnish

1 Combine the ginger, garlic, star anise, rice wine, soy sauce, and sesame oil in a bowl and stir in 5 tablespoons water. Place the chicken in a pan, add the spice mixture, and bring to a boil.

2 Transfer to the slow cooker, cover, and cook on low for 4 hours, or until the chicken is tender and cooked through.

3 Remove and discard the star anise. Transfer the chicken to warm plates and serve garnished with shredded scallions.

Cook's tip
Serve the chicken with plain boiled rice or egg noodles. However, remember that brown rice contains about five times as much fat as white rice.

Chicken Braised with Red Cabbage

This is a classic combination that is traditionally
served in the winter when red cabbage is in season.

◎ Serves 4

♨ Preparation time: 15 minutes, plus 10 minutes' pre-cooking

♡ Cooking time: 5 hours

Ingredients

2 tbsp sunflower oil

4 skinless chicken thighs or drumsticks

1 onion, chopped

5 1/2 cups shredded red cabbage

2 apples, peeled and chopped

12 canned or cooked chestnuts, halved (optional)

1/2 tsp juniper berries

1/2 cup red wine

salt and pepper

fresh flat-leaf parsley sprigs, to garnish

1 Heat the oil in a large, heavy pan. Add the chicken and cook, turning frequently, for 5 minutes until golden on all sides. Using a slotted spoon transfer to a plate lined with paper towels.

2 Add the onion to the pan and cook over medium heat, stirring occasionally, until softened. Stir in the cabbage and the apples and cook, stirring occasionally, for 5 minutes. Add the chestnuts, if using, juniper berries, and wine and season to taste with salt and pepper. Bring to a boil.

3 Spoon half the cabbage mixture into the slow cooker, add the chicken pieces, then top with the remaining cabbage mixture. Cover and cook on low for 5 hours until the chicken is tender and cooked through. Serve immediately, garnished with sprigs of parsley.

Cook's tip
If possible, stir the mixture about halfway through the
cooking time to make sure that all the cabbage is cooked
through. Replace the lid as soon as possible afterward—
and use oven mitts if the lid is hot.

CHIPOTLE CHICKEN

Chipotle chilies are smoked jalapeños and they impart a distinctive flavor to this dish, but remember that they are still hot.

Serves 4

Preparation time: 10 minutes, plus 30 minutes' soaking, plus 5–10 minutes to finish

Cooking time: 5 hours

Ingredients

4–6 chipotle chilies

4 garlic cloves, unpeeled

1 small onion, chopped

14 oz canned chopped tomatoes

1 ¼ cups hot chicken or
 vegetable stock

4 skinless chicken breast portions

salt and pepper

1 Preheat the oven to 400°F. Place the chilies in a bowl and pour in just enough hot water to cover. Set aside to soak for 30 minutes. Meanwhile, place the unpeeled garlic cloves on a cookie sheet and roast in the oven for about 10 minutes until soft. Remove from the oven and let cool.

2 Drain the chilies, reserving ½ cup of the soaking water. Seed the chilies, if you like, and chop coarsely. Place the chilies and reserved soaking water in a blender or food processor and process to a purée. Peel and mash the garlic in a bowl.

3 Place the chili purée, garlic, onion, and tomatoes in the slow cooker and stir in the stock. Season the chicken portions with salt and pepper and place them in the slow cooker. Cover and cook on low for about 5 hours until the chicken is tender and cooked through.

4 Lift the chicken out of the slow cooker with a slotted spoon, cover, and keep warm. Pour the cooking liquid into a pan and bring to a boil on the stove. Boil for 5–10 minutes until reduced. Place the chicken on warm plates, spoon the sauce over it, and serve.

Cook's tip
Breast is the leanest chicken meat and, if you're on a low-fat diet, you should always make sure it is skinless as this reduces the fat content considerably.

Variation
If you want to save preparation time, used canned chipotle chilies in adobo sauce. These don't need to be soaked and you can simply purée them with the sauce.

CARIBBEAN BEEF STEW

*Packed with flavor and bursting with color, this is a
perfect dish to come home to after a busy day.*

Serves 6

Preparation time: 20 minutes, plus 10 minutes' pre-cooking

Cooking time: 7½ hours

Ingredients

1 lb braising steak

3½ cups diced pumpkin or other squash

1 onion, chopped

1 red bell pepper, seeded and chopped

2 garlic cloves, finely chopped

1-inch piece fresh ginger root,
   finely chopped

1 tbsp sweet or hot paprika

1 cup beef stock

14 oz canned chopped tomatoes

14 oz canned pigeon peas,
   drained and rinsed

14 oz canned black-eyed peas,
   drained and rinsed

salt and pepper

1 Trim off any visible fat from the steak, then dice the meat. Heat a large, heavy pan without adding any
extra fat. Add the meat and cook, stirring constantly, for a few minutes until golden all over. Stir in the
pumpkin, onion, and bell pepper and cook for 1 minute, then add the spices, stock, and tomatoes, and
bring to a boil.

2 Transfer the mixture to the slow cooker, cover, and cook on low for 7 hours. Add the pigeon peas and
black-eyed peas to the stew and season to taste with salt and pepper. Re-cover and cook on high for
30 minutes, then serve.

Cook's tip
*Pigeon peas are also known as gunga peas, Jamaica
peas, and Congo peas. Light brown in color with darker
flecks, they are popular throughout the Caribbean. If you
can't find them, substitute canned garbanzo beans.*

MIXED BEAN CHILI

This colorful dish makes an economical and tasty
midweek supper when served with boiled rice.

Serves 4–6

Preparation time: 10 minutes, plus overnight soaking, plus 25 minutes' pre-cooking

Cooking time: 10 hours

Ingredients

2 tbsp corn oil

1 onion, chopped

1 garlic clove, finely chopped

1 fresh red chili, seeded and chopped

1 yellow bell pepper, seeded and chopped

1 tsp ground cumin

1 tbsp chili powder

2/3 cup dried red kidney beans, soaked overnight, drained, and rinsed

2/3 cup dried black beans, soaked overnight, drained, and rinsed

2/3 cup dried pinto beans, soaked overnight, drained, and rinsed

4 cups vegetable stock

1 tbsp sugar

salt and pepper

chopped fresh cilantro, to garnish

1 Heat the oil in a large, heavy pan. Add the onion, garlic, chili, and bell pepper and cook over medium heat, stirring occasionally, for 5 minutes. Stir in the cumin and chili powder and cook, stirring, for 1–2 minutes. Add the drained beans and stock and bring to a boil. Boil vigorously for 15 minutes.

2 Transfer the mixture to the slow cooker, cover, and cook on low for 10 hours until the beans are tender.

3 Season the mixture with salt and pepper, then ladle about one-third into a bowl. Mash well with a potato masher, then return the mashed beans to the cooker, and stir in the sugar. Serve immediately, sprinkled with chopped fresh cilantro.

Cook's tip
Both kidney beans and black beans contain a toxin
(pinto beans don't) that is destroyed by vigorous boiling.
It is important, therefore, that they are precooked
before being transferred to the slow cooker.

Variation
You can serve the beans sprinkled with diced, reduced-fat
cheese. Use about 4 oz in total.

WINTER VEGETABLE MEDLEY

This makes a great vegetarian main course, but also goes well with lean roast meat, such as chicken.

○ Serves 4

⚱ Preparation time: 15 minutes, plus 10 minutes' pre-cooking

🧤 Cooking time: 3 hours

Ingredients

2 tbsp sunflower oil

2 onions, chopped

3 carrots, chopped

3 parsnips, chopped

2 bunches celery, chopped, leaves reserved

2 tbsp chopped fresh parsley

1 tbsp chopped fresh cilantro

1 1/4 cups vegetable stock

salt and pepper

1 Heat the oil in a large, heavy pan. Add the onions and cook over medium heat, stirring occasionally, for 5 minutes until softened. Add the carrots, parsnips, and celery and cook, stirring occasionally, for 5 minutes more. Stir in the herbs, season with salt and pepper, and pour in the stock. Bring to a boil.

2 Transfer the vegetable mixture to the slow cooker, cover, and cook on high for 3 hours until tender. Taste and adjust the seasoning if necessary. Using a slotted spoon, transfer the medley to warm plates, then spoon over a little of the cooking liquid. Garnish with a few of the reserved celery leaves.

Cook's tip
Strain any leftover cooking liquid and store in the refrigerator or freezer to use as vegetable stock.

Variation
For a more substantial dish—with a slightly higher fat content—sprinkle thinly shaved Parmesan cheese over each portion or drizzle with 2 tablespoons heavy cream.

CHAPTER 4: EASY ENTERTAINING

BULGARIAN CHICKEN

East meets West in Bulgarian cuisine, as typified by the combination of sweet paprika and hot chili in this classic dish.

 Serves 6

Preparation time: 20 minutes, plus 10 minutes' pre-cooking

Cooking time: 6 hours

Ingredients

4 tbsp sunflower oil

6 chicken portions

2 onions, chopped

2 garlic cloves, finely chopped

1 fresh red chili, seeded and finely chopped

6 tomatoes, peeled and chopped

2 tsp sweet paprika

1 bay leaf

1 cup hot chicken stock

salt and pepper

fresh thyme sprigs, to garnish

1 Heat half the oil in a large, heavy skillet. Add the chicken portions and cook over medium heat, turning occasionally, for about 10 minutes, until golden all over.

2 Transfer the contents of the skillet to the slow cooker and add the onions, garlic, chili, and tomatoes. Sprinkle in the paprika, add the bay leaf, and pour in the stock. Season with salt and pepper. Stir well, cover, and cook on low for 6 hours until the chicken is cooked through and tender. Serve immediately, garnished with sprigs of thyme.

Cook's tip
The cooking time can vary depending on the size and type of the chicken portions. Test that the chicken is cooked through by piercing the thickest part with the point of a sharp knife. If the juices run clear, with no hint of pink, the chicken is cooked.

CHICKEN CACCIATORE

*Serve this traditional Italian dish with a crisp mixed salad
rather than pasta if you are following a low-carb diet.*

Serves 4

Preparation time: 20 minutes, plus 15 minutes' pre-cooking

Cooking time: 5 hours

Ingredients

3 tbsp olive oil

4 chicken portions, skinned

2 onions, sliced

2 garlic cloves, finely chopped

14 oz canned chopped tomatoes

1 tbsp tomato paste

2 tbsp chopped fresh parsley

2 tsp fresh thyme leaves

²⁄₃ cup red wine

salt and pepper

fresh thyme sprigs, to garnish

1 Heat the oil in a heavy skillet. Add the chicken portions and cook over medium heat, turning occasionally, for 10 minutes until golden all over. Using a slotted spoon, transfer the chicken to the slow cooker.

2 Add the onions to the skillet and cook, stirring occasionally, for 5 minutes until softened and just turning golden. Add the garlic, tomatoes and their can juices, tomato paste, parsley, thyme, and wine. Season with salt and pepper and bring to a boil.

3 Pour the tomato mixture over the chicken pieces. Cover and cook on low for 5 hours until the chicken is tender and cooked through. Taste and adjust the seasoning if necessary, and serve, garnished with sprigs of thyme.

Cook's tip
*Removing the skin from chicken before cooking
it reduces the fat content considerably.*

Variation
*You can also make this dish with turkey legs,
thighs, or supremes, all of which become
flavorful and juicy when cooked in this way.*

LAMB SHANKS WITH OLIVES

This is the perfect choice for slow cooking as the meat becomes melt-in-your-mouth tender and the flavors mingle superbly.

Serves 4

Preparation time: 15 minutes, plus 15 minutes' pre-cooking

Cooking time: 8½ hours

Ingredients

1½ tbsp all-purpose flour

4 lamb shanks

2 tbsp olive oil

1 onion, sliced

2 garlic cloves, finely chopped

2 tsp sweet paprika

14 oz canned chopped tomatoes

2 tbsp tomato paste

2 carrots, sliced

2 tsp sugar

1 cup red wine

2-inch cinnamon stick

2 fresh rosemary sprigs

1 cup pitted black olives

2 tbsp lemon juice

2 tbsp chopped fresh mint

salt and pepper

fresh mint sprigs, to garnish

1 Spread out the flour on a plate and season with salt and pepper. Toss the lamb in the seasoned flour and shake off any excess. Heat the oil in a large, heavy pan. Add the lamb shanks and cook over medium heat, turning frequently, for 6–8 minutes until browned all over. Transfer to a plate and set aside.

2 Add the onions and garlic to the pan and cook, stirring frequently, for 5 minutes until softened. Stir in the paprika and cook for 1 minute. Add the tomatoes, tomato paste, carrots, sugar, wine, cinnamon stick, and rosemary and bring to a boil.

3 Transfer the vegetable mixture to the slow cooker and add the lamb shanks. Cover and cook on low for 8 hours until the lamb is very tender.

4 Add the olives, lemon juice, and mint to the slow cooker. Re-cover and cook on high for 30 minutes. Remove and discard the rosemary and cinnamon and serve, garnished with mint sprigs.

Cook's tip
Lamb shanks are quite unwieldy things. Most medium-sized slow cookers, especially oval ones, can handle four, but if you're planning to cook for more people, check in advance that you have sufficient room.

Variation
You could substitute 1 lb 9 oz boneless shoulder of lamb for the lamb shanks. Trim off any excess fat and cut the meat into 2-inch cubes, then proceed as in the recipe.

SPRINGTIME LAMB WITH ASPARAGUS

Seasonal ingredients have a deliciously fresh flavor, but you can enjoy the taste of springtime at any time of year if you use frozen asparagus.

Serves 4

Preparation time: 20 minutes, plus 10 minutes' pre-cooking, plus 5 minutes to finish

Cooking time: $7\frac{1}{4}$ hours

Ingredients

2 tbsp sunflower oil

1 onion, thinly sliced

2 garlic cloves, very finely chopped

2 lb 4 oz boneless shoulder of lamb,
   cut into 1-inch cubes

8 oz asparagus spears, thawed if frozen

$1\frac{1}{4}$ cups chicken stock

4 tbsp lemon juice

$\frac{2}{3}$ cup heavy cream

salt and pepper

1 Heat the oil in a large, heavy skillet. Add the onion and cook over medium heat, stirring occasionally, for 5 minutes until softened. Add the garlic and lamb and cook, stirring occasionally, for 5 minutes more until the lamb is lightly browned all over.

2 Meanwhile, trim off and reserve the tips of the asparagus spears. Cut the stalks into 2–3 pieces. Add the stock and lemon juice to the skillet, season with salt and pepper, and bring to a boil. Lower the heat, add the asparagus stalks, and simmer for 2 minutes.

3 Transfer the mixture to the slow cooker. Cover and cook on low for 7 hours until the lamb is tender.

4 About 20 minutes before you intend to serve, cook the reserved asparagus tips in a pan of lightly salted, boiling water for 5 minutes. Drain well, then combine with the cream. Spoon the cream mixture on top of the lamb mixture but do not stir it in. Re-cover and cook on high for 15–20 minutes to heat through before serving.

Cook's tip
Lamb, particularly shoulder, is often quite fatty. Trim off as much fat as possible before dicing the meat to prevent a layer of grease from forming on top of the stew. If it does, spoon off as much as possible before adding the cream and asparagus mixture.

Variation
This dish also works well with veal with the bonus that stewing veal is usually inexpensive. It is a fairly lean meat with a special affinity with lemons and a delicate flavor that will be complemented by the asparagus cream sauce.

LAMB TAGINE

This North African combination of lamb, dried fruit, and nuts is delicately spiced and wonderfully rich in flavor.

🍽 Serves 6

🥣 Preparation time: 15 minutes, plus 10 minutes' pre-cooking

🧤 Cooking time: 8 1/2 hours

Ingredients

3 tbsp olive oil

2 red onions, chopped

2 garlic cloves, finely chopped

1-inch piece fresh ginger root, finely chopped

1 yellow bell pepper, seeded and chopped

2 lb 4 oz boneless shoulder of lamb, trimmed and cut into 1-inch cubes

3 3/4 cups lamb or chicken stock

1 cup no-soak dried apricots, halved

1 tbsp honey

4 tbsp lemon juice

pinch of saffron threads

2-inch cinnamon stick

salt and pepper

To garnish

1/2 cup sliced almonds, toasted

fresh cilantro sprigs

1 Heat the oil in a large, heavy pan. Add the onions, garlic, ginger, and bell pepper and cook over low heat, stirring occasionally, for 5 minutes until the onion has softened. Add the lamb and stir well to mix, then pour in the stock. Add the apricots, honey, lemon juice, saffron, and cinnamon stick and season with the salt and pepper. Bring to a boil.

2 Transfer the mixture to the slow cooker. Cover and cook on low for 8 1/2 hours until the meat is tender.

3 Remove and discard the cinnamon stick. Transfer to warm serving plates, sprinkle with the almonds, garnish with fresh cilantro, and serve.

JAMBALAYA

This Louisiana classic is thought to get its name from the French jambon or the Spanish jamón—meaning ham, which is a traditional ingredient.

Serves 6

Preparation time: 20 minutes, plus 15 minutes' pre-cooking

Cooking time: 6½ hours

Ingredients

½ tsp cayenne pepper

½ tsp freshly ground black pepper

1 tsp salt

2 tsp chopped fresh thyme

12 oz skinless, boneless chicken
  breasts, diced

2 tbsp corn oil

2 onions, chopped

2 garlic cloves, finely chopped

2 green bell peppers, seeded and chopped

2 celery stalks, chopped

⅔ cup chopped smoked ham

generous 1 cup sliced chorizo sausage

14 oz canned chopped tomatoes

2 tbsp tomato paste

1 cup chicken stock

1 lb peeled raw shrimp

2⅔ cups cooked rice

snipped fresh chives, to garnish

1 Combine the cayenne, black pepper, salt, and thyme in a bowl. Add the chicken and toss to coat. Heat the oil in a large, heavy pan. Add the onions, garlic, bell peppers, and celery and cook over low heat, stirring occasionally, for 5 minutes. Add the chicken and cook over medium heat, stirring frequently, for 5 minutes more until golden all over. Stir in the ham, chorizo, tomatoes, tomato paste, and stock and bring to a boil.

2 Transfer the mixture to the slow cooker. Cover and cook on low for 6 hours. Add the shrimp and rice, re-cover, and cook on high for 30 minutes.

3 Taste and adjust the seasoning, if necessary. Transfer to warm plates, garnish with chives, and serve the jambalaya immediately.

Cook's tip
Traditional recipes add raw rice toward the end of the cooking time. Using cooked rice makes this rather less hit-and-miss. Alternatively, just add the shrimp in step 2 and simply serve the jambalaya on a bed of freshly cooked rice.

BOEUF BOURGUIGNONNE

It is well worth buying a full-bodied, good-quality red wine—
preferably Burgundy—for this perennially popular French classic.

Serves 6

Preparation time: 15 minutes, plus 15 minutes' pre-cooking

Cooking time: 7¼ hours

Ingredients

1 cup diced bacon

2 tbsp all-purpose flour

2 lb braising steak, trimmed and cut into
   1-inch cubes

3 tbsp olive oil

2 tbsp sweet butter

12 pearl onions or shallots

2 garlic cloves, finely chopped

⅔ cup beef stock

2 cups full-bodied red wine

bouquet garni

2 cups sliced mushrooms

salt and pepper

1 Cook the bacon in a large, heavy pan, stirring occasionally, until the fat runs and the pieces are crisp. Meanwhile, spread out the flour on a plate and season with salt and pepper. Toss the steak cubes in the flour to coat, shaking off any excess. Using a slotted spoon, transfer the bacon to a plate. Add the oil to the pan. When it is hot, add the steak cubes and cook, in batches, stirring occasionally, for 5 minutes until browned all over. Transfer to the plate with a slotted spoon.

2 Add the butter to the pan. When it has melted, add the onions and garlic and cook, stirring occasionally, for 5 minutes. Return the bacon and steak to the pan and pour in the stock and wine. Bring to a boil.

3 Transfer the mixture to the slow cooker and add the bouquet garni. Cover and cook on low for 7 hours until the meat is tender.

4 Add the mushrooms to the slow cooker and stir well. Re-cover and cook on high for 15 minutes.

5 Remove and discard the bouquet garni. Adjust the seasoning if necessary, then serve immediately.

Cook's tip
Boeuf bourguignonne is even better served the next day. Leave to cool, then transfer to a suitable container, and store in the refrigerator. Skim off any fat from the surface and reheat in a large pan set over a low heat. Never reheat food in the slow cooker.

Variation
If the sauce looks too thin, add 1–2 tablespoons cornstarch mixed to a paste with a little water when you add the mushrooms. Stir it in well before replacing the lid.

DUCKLING WITH APPLES

As the duckling is braised gently, all the meat becomes deliciously tender, so you can use the whole bird for this tasty dish.

🍽 Serves 4

🥣 Preparation time: 15 minutes, plus 15 minutes' pre-cooking, plus 5 minutes to finish

🧤 Cooking time: 8 hours

Ingredients

4–4 lb 8 oz duckling, cut into 8 pieces

2 tbsp olive oil

1 onion, finely chopped

1 carrot, finely chopped

1 1/4 cups chicken stock

1 1/4 cups dry white wine

bouquet garni

1/4 cup sweet butter

4 eating apples

salt and pepper

1 Season the duckling pieces with salt and pepper. Heat the oil in a large, heavy skillet. Add all the duckling pieces, placing the breast portions skin side down. Cook over medium-high heat for a few minutes until golden brown, then transfer the breast portions to a plate. Turn the other pieces and continue to cook until browned all over. Transfer to the plate.

2 Add the onion and carrot to the skillet and cook over low heat, stirring occasionally, for 5 minutes until the onion is softened. Add the stock and wine and bring to a boil.

3 Transfer the vegetable mixture to the slow cooker. Add the duckling pieces and the bouquet garni. Cover and cook on low for 8 hours, occasionally skimming off the fat from the slow cooker and replacing the lid immediately each time.

4 Shortly before you are ready to serve, peel, core, and slice the apples. Melt the butter in a large skillet. Add the apple slices and cook over medium heat, turning occasionally, for 5 minutes until golden.

5 Spoon the cooked apples onto warm plates and divide the duckling among them. Skim off the fat and strain the sauce into a pitcher, then pour it over the duckling, and serve.

Cook's tip
Ready-made bouquets garnis, either resembling tea bags or tied in a square of cheesecloth, are available from supermarkets. If you want to use fresh herbs, tie together 3 parsley sprigs, 1 thyme sprig, and 1–2 bay leaves.

NEAPOLITAN BEEF

Most regions of Italy boast of their stufato—slow-braised beef—and, hardly surprisingly, in Naples the recipe includes tomatoes.

Serves 6

Preparation time: 15 minutes, plus 12 hours' marinating, plus 15 minutes' pre-cooking

Cooking time: 9 hours

Ingredients

1¼ cups red wine

4 tbsp olive oil

1 celery stalk, chopped

2 shallots, sliced

4 garlic cloves, finely chopped

1 bay leaf

10 fresh basil leaves

3 fresh parsley sprigs

pinch of grated nutmeg

pinch of ground cinnamon

2 cloves

3 lb 5 oz beef pot roast

1–2 garlic cloves, thinly sliced

⅓ cup chopped bacon or pancetta

14 oz canned chopped tomatoes

2 tbsp tomato paste

salt and pepper

1 Combine the wine, 2 tablespoons of the olive oil, the celery, shallots, garlic, herbs, and spices in a large, nonmetallic bowl. Add the beef, cover, and marinate, turning occasionally, for 12 hours.

2 Drain the beef, reserving the marinade, and pat dry with paper towels. Make small incisions all over the beef using a sharp knife. Insert a slice of garlic and a piece of bacon in each "pocket." Heat the remaining oil in a large skillet. Add the meat and cook over medium heat, turning frequently, until browned all over. Transfer the beef to the slow cooker.

3 Strain the reserved marinade into the skillet and bring to a boil. Stir in the tomatoes and tomato paste. Stir well, then pour the mixture over the beef. Cover and cook on low for about 9 hours until tender. If possible, turn the beef over halfway through the cooking time and re-cove the slow cooker immediately. To serve, remove the beef and place on a carving board. Cover with foil and let stand for 10–15 minutes to firm up. Cut into slices and transfer to a platter. Spoon the sauce over it and serve immediately.

SWEET-AND-SOUR SICILIAN PASTA

This colorful vegetarian sauce is a little like the classic French dish ratatouille but has an extra tang of balsamic vinegar and lemon juice.

Serves 4

Preparation time: 15 minutes, plus 15 minutes' pre-cooking

Cooking time: 5 hours

Ingredients

4 tbsp olive oil

1 large red onion, sliced

2 garlic cloves, finely chopped

2 red bell peppers, seeded and sliced

2 zucchini, cut into batons

1 eggplant, cut into batons

2 cups bottled strained tomatoes

4 tbsp lemon juice

2 tbsp balsamic vinegar

1/2 cup pitted black olives, sliced

1 tbsp sugar

14 oz dried fettuccine

salt and pepper

fresh flat-leaf parsley sprigs, to garnish

1 Heat the oil in a large, heavy pan. Add the onion, garlic, and bell peppers and cook over low heat, stirring occasionally, for 5 minutes. Add the zucchini and eggplant and cook, stirring occasionally, for 5 minutes more. Stir in the strained tomatoes and 2/3 cup water and bring to a boil. Stir in the lemon juice, vinegar, olives, and sugar and season with salt and pepper.

2 Transfer the mixture to the slow cooker. Cover and cook on low for 5 hours until all the vegetables are tender.

3 To cook the pasta, bring a large pan of lightly salted water to a boil. Add the fettuccine and bring back to a boil. Cook for 10–12 minutes until the pasta is tender but still firm to the bite. Drain and transfer to a warm serving dish. Spoon the vegetable mixture over the pasta, toss lightly, garnish with parsley, and serve.

Cook's tip

When cooking any type of pasta, make sure that the water is boiling, not merely simmering. This prevents the ribbons or strands from sticking together.

BOUILLABAISSE

This is only one, although perhaps the most famous, of Mediterranean
fish soups. For the best flavor, it should include a variety of different fish.

 Serves 6

Preparation time: 45 minutes

Cooking time: 8½ hours

Ingredients

5 lb mixed white fish, such as red snapper, porgy,
    sea bass, monkfish and whiting, filleted and
    bones and heads reserved, if possible

1 lb raw shrimp

grated rind of 1 orange

pinch of saffron threads

4 garlic cloves, finely chopped

1 cup olive oil

2 onions, finely chopped

1 leek, thinly sliced

4 potatoes, thinly sliced

2 large tomatoes, peeled and chopped

1 bunch fresh flat-leaf parsley, chopped

1 fresh fennel sprig

1 fresh thyme sprig

1 bay leaf

2 cloves

6 black peppercorns

1 strip orange rind

sea salt

crusty bread or croûtes, to serve

1 Cut the fish fillets into bitesized pieces and peel and devein the shrimp. Reserve the heads and shells
of the shrimp. Rinse the fish bones, if using, and cut off the gills of any fish heads. Place the chunks of
fish and the shrimp in a large bowl. Sprinkle with the grated orange rind, saffron, half the garlic, and
2 tablespoons of the oil. Cover and set aside in the refrigerator.

2 Put the remaining garlic, the onions, leek, potatoes, tomatoes, parsley, fennel, thyme, bay leaf, cloves,
peppercorns, and strip of orange rind in the slow cooker. Add the fish heads and bones, if using, and
the shrimp shells and heads. Pour in the remaining olive oil and 12½ cups boiling water or enough to
cover the ingredients by 1 inch/2.5 cm. Season with sea salt. Cover and cook on low for 8 hours.

3 Strain the stock and return the liquid to the slow cooker. Discard the flavorings, fish and shrimp trimmings but
retain the vegetables and return them to the slow cooker if you like. Add the fish and shrimp mixture, re-cover,
and cook on high for 30 minutes until the fish is cooked through and flakes easily with the point of a knife.

4 Ladle into warm bowls and serve with crusty bread or croûtes.

MOROCCAN SEA BASS

Delicate North African spices complement the delicious flavor of this attractive fish which is usually cooked whole.

Serves 2

Preparation time: 15 minutes, plus 10 minutes' pre-cooking, plus 5 minutes to finish

Cooking time: 6½–6¾ hours

Ingredients

2 tbsp olive oil

2 onions, chopped

2 garlic cloves, finely chopped

2 carrots, finely chopped

1 fennel bulb, finely chopped

½ tsp ground cumin

½ tsp ground cloves

1 tsp ground coriander

pinch of saffron threads

1¼ cups fish stock

1 preserved or fresh lemon

2-lb sea bass, cleaned

salt and pepper

1 Heat the oil in a large, heavy pan. Add the onions, garlic, carrots, and fennel and cook over medium heat, stirring occasionally, for 5 minutes. Stir in all the spices and cook, stirring, for 2 minutes more. Pour in the stock, season with salt and pepper, and bring to a boil.

2 Transfer the mixture to the slow cooker. Cover and cook on low for 6 hours or until the vegetables are tender.

3 Rinse the preserved lemon if using. Discard the fish head if you like. Slice the lemon and place the slices in the fish cavity, then place the fish in the slow cooker. Re-cover and cook on high for 30–45 minutes until the flesh flakes easily with the point of a knife.

4 Carefully transfer the fish to a platter and spoon the vegetables around it. Cover and keep warm. Transfer the cooking liquid to a pan and boil for a few minutes until reduced. Spoon it over the fish and serve.

Cook's tip
Before cooking the sea bass, cut off the sharply spined fins and scale it. This recipe also works extremely well with red snapper.

CABBAGE ROULADES WITH TOMATO SAUCE

These tasty stuffed cabbage rolls make a great vegetarian main course but can also be served as an appetizer, in which case make half the quantity.

Serves 6

Preparation time: 25 minutes, plus 20 minutes' pre-cooking

Cooking time: 3–4 hours

Ingredients

1 cup mixed nuts, finely ground

2 onions, finely chopped

1 garlic clove, finely chopped

2 celery stalks, finely chopped

1 cup grated Cheddar cheese

1 tsp finely chopped thyme

2 eggs

1 tsp yeast extract

12 large green cabbage leaves

Tomato sauce

2 tbsp sunflower oil

2 onions, chopped

2 garlic cloves, finely chopped

1 lb 5 oz canned
  chopped tomatoes

2 tbsp tomato sauce

1½ tsp sugar

1 bay leaf

salt and pepper

1 First make the tomato sauce. Heat the oil in a heavy pan. Add the onion and cook over medium heat, stirring occasionally, for 5 minutes until softened. Stir in the garlic and cook for 1 minute, then add the tomatoes, tomato paste, sugar, and bay leaf. Season with salt and pepper and bring to a boil. Lower the heat and simmer gently for 20 minutes until thickened.

2 Meanwhile, combine the nuts, onions, garlic, celery, cheese, and thyme in a bowl. Lightly beat the eggs with the yeast extract in a pitcher, then stir into the nut mixture. Set aside.

3 Cut out the thick stalk from the cabbage leaves. Blanch the leaves in a large pan of boiling water for 5 minutes, then drain, and refresh under cold water. Pat dry with paper towels.

4 Place a little of the nut mixture on the stalk end of each cabbage leaf. Fold the sides over, then roll up to make a neat packet.

5 Arrange the packets in the slow cooker, seam side down. Remove and discard the bay leaf from the tomato sauce and pour the sauce over the cabbage rolls. Cover and cook on low for 3–4 hours. Serve the cabbage roulades hot or cold.

EGGPLANT TIMBALES

Served with a quick and easy sauce and a salad, these attractive molds make an unusual vegetarian main course.

 Serves 4

Preparation time: 15 minutes, plus 20–25 minutes' pre-cooking

Cooking time: 2 hours

Ingredients

2 eggplant

3 tbsp olive oil, plus extra for greasing

2 onions, finely chopped

2 red bell peppers, seeded and chopped

1 large tomato, peeled and chopped

6 tbsp milk

2 egg yolks

pinch of ground cinnamon

1 cup finely crushed crispbread crumbs

salt and pepper

fresh cilantro sprigs, to garnish

For the sauce

1 1/4 cups sour cream

3–4 tbsp sun-dried tomato paste (optional)

1 Halve the eggplant and scoop out the flesh with a spoon. Reserve the shells and dice the flesh. Heat the oil in a large, heavy skillet. Add the onions and cook over low heat, stirring occasionally, for 5 minutes. Add the diced eggplant, bell peppers, and tomato and cook, stirring occasionally, for 15–20 minutes until all the vegetables are soft. Remove the skillet from the heat.

2 Transfer the mixture to a food processor or blender and process to a purée, then scrape into a bowl. Beat together the milk, egg yolks, cinnamon, and salt and pepper in a pitcher, then stir into the vegetable purée.

3 Brush 4 ramekins or cups with oil and sprinkle with the crispbread crumbs to coat. Tip out any excess. Mix about three-quarters of the remaining crumbs into the vegetable purée. Slice the eggplant shells into strips and use them to line the ramekins, leaving the ends protruding above the rims. Spoon the filling into the ramekins, sprinkle with the remaining crumbs, and fold the overlapping ends over.

4 Cover with foil and place in the slow cooker. Pour in sufficient boiling water to come about one-third of the way up the sides of the ramekins. Cover and cook on high for 2 hours.

5 To make the sauce, lightly beat the sour cream and add the tomato paste to taste, if desired. Season with salt and pepper. Lift the ramekins out of the cooker and remove the foil. Invert onto serving plates and serve with the sauce, garnished with cilantro sprigs.

CHAPTER 5: DESSERTS

MAGIC LEMON SPONGE

This deliciously tangy dessert is a good, old-fashioned family favorite
that looks and smells tempting and tastes scrumptious.

 Serves 4

Preparation time: 20 minutes

Cooking time: 2½ hours

Ingredients

¾ cup superfine sugar

3 eggs, separated

1¼ cups milk

3 tbsp self-rising flour, sifted

⅔ cup freshly squeezed lemon juice

confectioner's sugar, for dusting

1 Beat the sugar with the egg yolks in a bowl, using an electric mixer. Gradually beat in the milk, followed by the flour and the lemon juice.

2 Whisk the egg whites in a separate, grease-free bowl until stiff. Fold half the whites into the yolk mixture using a rubber or plastic spatula in a figure -eight movement, then fold in the remainder. Try not to knock out the air.

3 Pour the mixture into an ovenproof dish, cover with foil, and place in the slow cooker. Add sufficient boiling water to come about one-third of the way up the side of the dish. Cover and cook on high for 2½ hours until the mixture has set and the sauce and sponge have separated.

4 Lift the dish out of the cooker and discard the foil. Lightly sift a little icing sugar over the top and serve.

Cook's tip
Don't worry if the mixture looks as if it is slightly curdled
after you have folded in the egg whites. It will be all right.

APPLE CRUMBLE

Served hot or cold, on its own or accompanied by cream, yogurt, or ice cream, this is always a sure-fire family favorite.

Serves 4

Preparation time: 15 minutes

Cooking time: 5½ hours

Ingredients

½ cup all-purpose flour

½ cup rolled oats

⅔ cup brown sugar

½ tsp grated nutmeg

½ tsp ground cinnamon

1 cup butter, softened

4 cooking apples, peeled, cored, and sliced

4–5 tbsp apple juice

1 Sift the flour into a bowl and stir in the oats, sugar, nutmeg, and cinnamon. Add the butter and mix in with a pastry blender or the prongs of a fork.

2 Place the apple slices in the base of the slow cooker and add the apple juice. Sprinkle the flour mixture evenly over them.

3 Cover and cook on low for 5½ hours. Serve hot, warm or cold.

Cook's tip
Ground nutmeg loses its aroma and flavor very quickly. It is better to buy whole nutmegs and grate them freshly just before using.

Variation
Sprinkle scant ½ cup mixed dried fruit over the apple slices before adding the crumble topping.

THAI BLACK RICE PUDDING

*Glutinous or sticky rice is very popular in Thailand. The black
variety has an unusual, nutty flavor and looks intriguing.*

Serves 4

Preparation time: 5 minutes, plus 15 minutes' pre-cooking

Cooking time: 2–2½ hours

Ingredients

scant 1 cup black glutinous rice

2 tbsp light brown sugar

2 cups canned coconut milk

3 eggs

2 tbsp superfine sugar

1 Combine the rice, brown sugar, and half the coconut milk
in a pan, then stir in 1 cup water. Bring to a boil, then
reduce the heat, and simmer, stirring occasionally, for
15 minutes until almost all the liquid has been absorbed.
Transfer the mixture to a heatproof dish or to ramekins.

2 Lightly beat the eggs with the remaining coconut milk and
the superfine sugar. Strain the mixture over the rice.

3 Cover with foil and place the dish in the slow cooker.
Pour in enough boiling water to come about one-third of the
way up the side of the dish. Cover and cook on high for
2–2½ hours until set. Remove the dish from the cooker and
discard the foil before serving either hot or cold.

Cook's tip
*Both black and white glutinous rice are available
from many supermarkets and Asian food stores.*

Variation
*This dish is particularly refreshing and attractive
if served with slices of fresh mango fanned out
on the plates beside it.*

BLUSHING PEARS

This easy, yet very appealing dessert is great for dinner parties but not really suitable for serving to children.

🍽 Serves 6

🥣 Preparation time: 15 minutes, plus cooling and chilling

🧤 Cooking time: 4 hours

Ingredients

6 small ripe pears

1 cup ruby port

1 cup superfine sugar

1 tsp finely chopped candied ginger

2 tbsp lemon juice

whipped cream or strained plain yogurt, to serve

1 Peel the pears, cut them in half lengthwise, and scoop out the cores. Place them in the slow cooker.

2 Combine the port, sugar, ginger, and lemon juice in a pitcher and pour the mixture over the pears. Cover and cook on low for 4 hours until the pears are tender.

3 Leave the pears to cool in the slow cooker, then carefully transfer to a bowl, and chill in the refrigerator until required.

4 To serve, partially cut each pear half into about 6 slices lengthwise, leaving the fruit intact at the stalk end. Carefully lift the pear halves onto serving plates and press gently to fan out the slices. Serve with whipped cream or yogurt.

Cook's tip
The easiest way to scoop out the cores from the pear halves is with a melon baller.

Variation
If you substitute medium white wine for the port, the dessert won't be so colorful, but it will taste equally delicious.

ITALIAN BREAD PUDDING

This is a sophisticated version of the popular pudding using panettone, a light-textured Italian Christmas cake flavored with citrus rind and golden raisins.

Serves 6

Preparation time: 20 minutes, plus cooling and chilling

Cooking time: 2½ hours

Ingredients

sweet butter, for greasing

6 slices panettone

3 tbsp Marsala wine

1¼ cups milk

1¼ cups light cream

½ cup superfine sugar

grated rind of ½ lemon

pinch of ground cinnamon

3 extra large eggs, lightly beaten

heavy cream, to serve

1 Grease a heatproof bowl and set aside. Place the panettone on a deep plate and sprinkle with the Marsala wine.

2 Pour the milk and cream into a pan and add the sugar, lemon rind, and cinnamon. Gradually bring to boil over low heat, stirring until the sugar has dissolved. Remove the pan from the heat and let cool slightly, then pour the mixture onto the eggs, beating constantly.

3 Place the panettone in the prepared bowl, pour in the egg mixture and cover with foil. Place in the slow cooker and add enough boiling water to come about one-third of the way up the side of the bowl. Cover and cook on high for 2½ hours until set.

4 Remove the bowl from the slow cooker and discard the foil. Let cool, then chill in the refrigerator until required. Loosen the sides of the pudding with a knife and turn out onto a serving dish. Serve with cream on the side.

Cook's tip
A 4-cup bowl gives the best shape for turning out, but if you don't have one, cook and serve the pudding in an ordinary ovenproof dish.

Variation
Panettone is widely available from supermarkets and Italian delicatessens, especially at Christmas time. However, if you can't find it, substitute slices of a light fruit loaf.

INDEX